10 Things I Wish Someone Would've Told Me Before I Started Selling Drugs

By

Vince Evans

Table of Contents

Preface

I'm writing this book for the sole purpose of saving lives. This is not something to be taken lightly. If you are a young person growing up in the inner-city, or someone who genuinely cares for a young person growing up in the inner-city, then I hope and pray that you will take heed to what I'm about to share with you in this short book.

I started selling drugs at an early age, weed at 12 and cocaine at 13. Before becoming an adult, I was already in prison serving a LIFE sentence. If only someone would have took the time to tell me some of the things that I'm about to share with you, maybe I would have made different choices and enjoyed my youth more. No one sat me down and told me the truth about the so-called dope game and what it would eventually do to me, so I dove in head-first and learned the hard way.

The truth of the matter is that we live in a culture of instant gratification, meaning we want things immediately. The fast cash that comes from selling drugs has a certain type of appeal to young people in the ghetto, which is why so many admire, if not embrace, the drug dealing lifestyle. It's time to start pointing out the value of delayed gratification, working toward long-run payoffs instead of chasing a few dollars in the moment.

If nothing else, I would like to use this book to shed some light on the dark side of selling drugs, the part that is rarely exposed in rap lyrics and hood novels. I can promise that if you take the time to read what I share here, you will see things a little differently and be better equipped to do things differently as well. It only takes one person to create change, so let's change some lives!

Chapter 1: "You Will Become An Urban Terrorist!"

Nobody bothered to tell me that my decision to sell drugs would change the way the people in my neighborhood looked at me. I went from being the sweet kid with good manners to being the wild teenager with no respect for anyone or anything. The same people who once sent me to the store for them suddenly crossed the street to avoid interacting with me and I didn't even care. I was all about making money, so everything else was irrelevant.

When you sell drugs, you become an urban terrorist because your lifestyle terrorizes your community. Residents live in fear of the violence that accompanies drug dealing, everything from simple robbery to multiple murders could very easily be lurking right around the corner.

Law-abiding citizens grow to fear and despise drug dealers because they see drug-dealing as evil and dealers as promoters of that evil. They may have known you since the day you were born, but when they see you conducting a drug transaction, they start wondering if they ever really knew you at all. They no longer feel safe in your presence so they find themselves avoiding you at any and all cost.

As you become more and more focused on getting your money, you fail to recognize what you're doing to the community, especially the kids who are right underneath you in age. You're exposing them to things they should be sheltered from, things like guns, drugs, sex, and violence. It's no wonder why parents look at you with fear and contempt in their eyes!

While you're on the block smoking blunts, popping bottles, flashing guns, and basically wreaking havoc, the residents are trying their best to stay out of your way. No one wants to be robbed by one of your customers or cradle the head of a dying child who caught a bullet that was intended for you. So not only are you feared, but you're also despised because of what you do and what it has the potential to bring upon the innocent residents around you.

As a drug dealer you also become mortal enemies with law enforcement officers. When you see them coming, you have to get away. When they see you easing off, they have to investigate by pursuing you. They have a job to do, which is to arrest criminals, and despite the corruption that runs rampant throughout many police departments in this day and age, you are still a criminal if you sell drugs. So the police feel justified in hunting you down like a wild animal whenever they catch you out and about, and the community is often torn between wanting you to be safe from police brutality and wanting the police to get you off the streets.

Until you find yourself running through backyards in the middle of the night with trigger-happy police right on your heels, you can't even begin to understand the fear that accompanies situations of that nature. Yeah, it's a natural response to be afraid when your enemy is pursuing you with a strength and determination similar to that of a professional athlete. In those moments, you wonder what it's all for and you may even ask God to help you even though you know you don't deserve it.

In short, as a drug dealer, you are a liability to your community, not an asset. You prey on the misery of others by capitalizing on their addiction. You bring drama, beef, and war into neighborhoods where decent people are trying to raise families. You are hated, not loved.

Nobody told me any of this, which is why I was delusional about my relationship with the neighborhood. I was shocked to learn of the overall relief that resonated through the community once I was arrested, sentenced, and shipped off to the penitentiary. But at the end of the day, a part of me acknowledged the fact that I was exactly where I was supposed to be, caged up like the animal that I had become!

Chapter 2: "Addicts Will Constantly Try To Take Advantage Of You And Get Over On You!"

Nobody bothered to tell me that my decision to sell drugs would place me in situations where addicts would constantly be plotting and scheming against me in order to secure their high. If I had a dime for every time a customer told me a lie in hopes of getting drugs from me for free, I'd be rich. If I had a penny for every time a customer gave me short money claiming it was more than it really was, I'd have a nice retirement nest egg.

When you sell drugs, you get a front row seat to the full scale of addiction. You see some things that will change your outlook on life and you do some things that will change the way you view yourself. Addiction makes people do crazy things and you condone it, even through your silence. Drug addicts will humiliate themselves in order to feed their habit, so why would you expect them to be honest with you?

Addicts tend to rely on running game and having slick mouthpieces, which means they believe in conning drug dealers out of drugs by using the gift of gab. Sometimes it works, but most of the time their intentions are clear and they end up with nothing. You will hear all types of sob stories and false promises, but the end result is that they will be asking you for drugs at a discounted rate, on credit, or for free. Oh yeah, the female addicts will occasionally attempt to trade sexual favors, while the male addicts more often than not barter stolen goods of some sort.

It may seem interesting and even challenging to decipher an addict's fast talk at first, but after a while it becomes a headache. Imagine listening to someone explain a problem in detail for ten minutes without stopping to take a breath, knowing that it will all lead to a request for some free drugs by the end.

Drug dealing is a constant negotiation, a battle of wills between desperate addicts and greedy dealers. By the end of the transaction, somebody has to win and someone has to lose. There's no such thing as mutual satisfaction in this arena. It's basically a struggle to find out who becomes the predator and who becomes prey.

There is no peace-of-mind for the drug dealer when transactions are being made because the customers desire to get over requires the dealer's full attention in order for the deal to be a profitable one. So living in a constant state of heightened suspicion is stressful and extremely unhealthy.

Nobody told me any of this, which is why I foolishly welcomed the back and forth dialogue between myself and the addicts who wanted what I had. In hindsight, I now realize how much time and energy was wasted during those verbal exchanges with people who were nothing more than parasites, and I was no better than them.

Chapter 3: "You Will Eventually Start Living Like The Same Addicts You Look Down On!"

Nobody bothered to tell me that my decision to sell drugs would eventually make it difficult to recognize that there was very little difference between myself and the people I sold drugs to. I recall making a vow to remain on the block until I turned my $40 into $1000, which meant eating, sleeping, and even using the bathroom right there. In order to accomplish my goal, I had to neglect my personal hygiene, not bathing properly or changing my clothes. I also had to spend the majority of my time in the presence of drug addicts, hanging out with them, interacting with them, and dealing with them. It took me about a week to achieve the goal, but I'm sure someone on the outside looking in lost the ability to distinguish me from the addicts who were my customers.

When you sell drugs, you adopt some characteristics and qualities of addicts. Your addiction to the pursuit of money causes you to embrace a twisted value system that can easily mirror the value system of a drug addict. While a drug addict's mission is to acquire drugs by whatever means are necessary, your agenda is to sell your drugs and stack up your money by whatever means are necessary. So if you have to be out on the block all night long without washing up or brushing your teeth, then so be it, as long as you have the money to show for it when the sun comes up.

Drug dealers who spend lots of time with addicts tend to listen to the stories told by the addicts. Those stories, more often than not, contain small amounts of what passes for wisdom in the eyes of people who do not have exposure to other ideas and outlooks. So addicts who colorfully express twisted views and distorted values, unintentionally influence the mentalities of the dealers who listen to them because the dealers are unconsciously seeking guidance.

Even if dealers do not really respect addicts, there's an unwritten rule to pay attention to what addicts say during moments of clarity because addicts have travelled down paths that dealers desperately want to avoid. But in the midst of this attentiveness, nonsense is pushed off as wise words and slick talk masquerades as good game.

While addicts justify their addiction to drugs, dealers justify their addiction to hustling. Truth is, there's no right way to do anything that's wrong, so there is no way to justify selling drugs. Just like there is no way to justify putting drugs into your body knowing that those drugs are destroying you physically. By engaging in destructive behavior on a regular basis, drug dealers are placing themselves in harm's way unnecessarily and putting their freedom, not to mention their lives, at risk every single time they make a transaction.

Drug addicts tend to be very inconsiderate of others. They often lie, steal, and cheat in order to get high. Drug dealers sometimes will lie, steal, and cheat in order to obtain drugs too. The only difference is that addicts chase a drug-induced high while dealers chase a drug-related high, the rush that comes from making fast money.

Nobody told me any of this, which is why I so easily embraced a value system similar to that of drug addicts. When I look back at my past realistically, I see that I was a lot like the customers I sold drugs to. And if I'm being completely honest, it embarrasses me a great deal to know that I was too blinded by the money to see what I had

become!

Chapter 4: "You Will See Adults You Love And Respect Fall Victim To Drugs And Become Shells Of Their Former Selves!"

Nobody bothered to tell me that my decision to sell drugs would cause me to watch many of my role models become weak versions of themselves. The crack epidemic hit my neighborhood, my community, my city, my state, and my country very hard. No household that I knew of was unaffected by it and no family that I was aware of escaped its impact. Relatives, friends of the family, neighbors, and familiar neighborhood residents all fell victim to the epidemic in one way or another. Mothers and fathers got addicted, aunts and uncles got addicted. Sisters and brothers got addicted. Nobody was immune, nobody was spared, not for real. As a drug dealer, I watched firsthand as many of the people I looked up to start getting high and losing their way. Strong men and women suddenly became desperate beggars and petty thieves, humbling themselves to me and pleading for my help as they scraped up a few dollars for their next high.

When you sell drugs for any extended period of time, you are destined to see someone deteriorate into a state of weakness that seemed impossible for them to reach from their previous state. Successful professionals in expensive cars allow their addiction to strip them of everything from their material possessions to their basic pride. One day they have it all, then the next day they have absolutely nothing.

As a drug dealer, you constantly witness the downfall of people who once stood tall. You watch as their addiction takes hold of them physically, mentally, emotionally, financially, and even spiritually. Physically, they lose weight and their personal hygiene declines. Mentally, their thoughts revolve around ways to get drugs and get high. Emotionally, they become selfish and stop caring deeply for others. Financially, they spend more and more money getting high until they reach the point where every penny they get is allocated toward purchasing drugs. Spiritually, their drug of choice becomes their God, receiving all of their dedication and devotion because the high becomes their heaven-on-earth.

So you may be wondering what that has to do with drug dealers, right? Well, addicts are usually someone's something. Every customer is somebody's relative, friend, neighbor, coworker, etc. Drug dealers are not exempt. A drug dealer's loved ones are just as susceptible to addictions anyone else and nothing hurts worse than when a drug dealer discovers that somebody near and dear to his/her heart has fallen victim to addiction.

I watched addiction destroy many of my loved ones. Some were able to make it out with scars and powerful testimonies, while others simply became consumed by drugs and ended up traveling down dead-end streets that had no outlets. A few are now in graves, but some are above ground living life as nothing more than zombies, walking around dead without even realizing it.

Drug dealers will witness career-oriented individuals spiral downward right before their very eyes. Addicts will go from driving luxury cars, to driving raggedy cars. They will go from driving raggedy cars, to riding bikes. They will go from riding bikes, to walking. They will go from walking, to standing around on corners.

Drug dealers will witness attractive women become hideous looking bags of skin and bone. Beautiful smiles will become rotten caves and voluptuous bodies will become disease-infested skeletons. When women run out of money, they will sometimes trade sexual favors for drugs. Drug dealers will not only witness the degradation, but more often than not they will actively participate in it.

Nobody told me any of this, which is why I so willingly sold drugs to any and every man and woman who wanted to buy them. As crack destroyed the people in my neighborhood, I lost my way and became an instrument of destruction myself, destroying lives and futures in the name of cash money!

Chapter 5: "Many Of The People In Your Life Will Have Hidden Agendas And Ulterior Motives!"

Nobody bothered to tell me that my decision to sell drugs would cause me to lose the ability to fully trust the people around me. I often looked into the smiling faces of family members, close friends, girlfriends, neighbors, and many others, not knowing if the smiles were real or fake. You see, as a drug dealer I was able to be what people near me wanted (and sometimes needed) me to be, so they would put up with my flaws in order to remain in my good graces. I understood the fact that not everyone in my life was genuine, but it would take incarceration for me to truly recognize who was authentic and who was not.

When you sell drugs, you have the potential to be an asset to the people around you. Knowing this, people will attempt to get close to you in order to benefit from what you're doing. Family members who don't miss a Sunday in church will overlook the fact that you're a drug dealer when they need a little extra money for bills or groceries. Friends will ignore your personality flaws when they need you to have their back in the heat of the moment. Females will lower their standards and hook up with you if they believe that you will cater to them financially or shower them with material gifts. So in the midst of all the people who are trying to be in your life, it becomes difficult to figure out who really likes you for you and who is simply along for the ride.

Some family members will profess undying love and devotion while secretly despising what you do for a living. However, they will gladly accept the ill-gotten fruits of your labor despite their "holier than thou" attitudes since bill collectors don't make distinctions between legitimate money and ill-gained money.

Some friends will base their friendship with you on certain predetermined conditions. For instance, a friend may be down to ride as long as you're paying for everything, but as soon as you experience a financial setback that same friend is nowhere to be found.

When you're a flashy drug dealer, females will gravitate toward you, especially gold-diggers. It will be hard to determine which ones like you and which ones just like the lifestyle that you live. If you're like most drug dealers, you won't really care for real as long as you're getting what you want from the, which is usually sex and quality time when you want it.

Not all relationships are tainted when you sell drugs, but many are. So you have to study people and be skeptical of their intentions. There is very little room for the type of unconditional trust that forms the foundation of healthy relationships, so the majority of your personal bonds with people are conditional and dependent on just how much you're willing to let your guard down.

Nobody told me any of this, which is why I was loyal to people who did not deserve my loyalty and I was disappointed by people who turned out to have hidden agendas and ulterior motives while interacting with me. Once I was stripped of my drug dealing status and my freedom, the truth about everyone in my life came out into the light. Like the old adage states, when you cut down the grass, you can see the snakes clearly. What I failed to realize was the fact that I was a snake as well!

Chapter 6: "The More You Have, The More People Will Want To Take It Away From You!"

Nobody bothered to tell me that my decision to sell drugs would breed jealousy and envy as I progressed toward so-called success. While my quality of life improved due to the profits that I made from drug dealing, I noticed how a wide variety of people suddenly wanted what I had. I quickly became cautious and somewhat paranoid because I was not sure who I could trust.

When you become a drug dealer and start experiencing financial gain that reveals itself through the things that you purchase and showcase to the world, certain types of people take notice. No matter how inconspicuous you believe you're being, there's always someone watching your every move very closely, looking for an opportunity to come for what you have.

Flaunting your ill-gained wealth draws the attention of robbers, men and women who wait patiently for opportunities to run up on you and figure out how to take a portion of the money and drugs you've stacked up, if not all of it. These robbers lay in the cut watching how you party, how you relax, how you hustle, and where you like to go regularly, in hopes of finding the perfect chance to catch you in a vulnerable state. Vulnerable states are often exploited through armed robberies, home invasions, kidnappings, and/or various combinations of the aforementioned tactics. It all ends with someone else walking away with the things that you place value on as a drug dealer.

Aside from illegal robberies, there are also robberies that are carried out somewhat legally due to your occupational choice. Between crooked police who extort you by continuously going in your pockets, and money hungry retailers who overcharge you for merchandise because they know you can afford it, you really don't stand a chance of holding on to the money that you make. Even if you somehow stack it up, you know in the back of your mind that law enforcement agencies will eventually be coming for it once your name starts coming up too much.

I always tell young aspiring drug dealers to choose another profession because selling drugs is a costly enterprise. Even if you make a lot of money, you always run the risk of catching a case and having to spend that money fighting for your freedom in a courtroom. And if you happen to lose that fight, you end up in prison while someone else controls your money if there's any left after the lawyer gets paid.

Once again I have to mention family members who feel like you owe them something for being related to them. They will criticize the way you make your money, but turn right around and ask for some of it when they need a little help financially. They tend to accept what you give them without complaint, until they feel comfortable enough to resume their never-ending criticism of the choices you've made in life.

Last but not least is the female who uses love and/or sex to subtly rob you. She praises everything you do as long as she can go shopping and keep a few dollars of your dirty money in her purse. As soon as you get too comfortable with her, she tends to take advantage by setting you up for a major loss. She might convince you to make an expensive purchase for her, or she might simply help a robber set you up. Either way, she will leave her relationship with you a little more financially secure than she was when she entered it. Plus, if you go to jail and leave your money with her, there is a very strong possibility that she will eventually begin to view that money as *HER* money.

Nobody told me any of this, so I ended up learning it the hard way. I was robbed by so many people, in so many different ways, it didn't make sense. The more I acquired, the more I felt like I was being circled by vultures. What slipped my mind was the fact that I was a vulture myself!

Chapter 7: "Older Hustlers Will Envy Your Rise And Applaud Your Downfall!"

Nobody bothered to tell me that my decision to sell drugs would cause the people I looked up to in the streets to become the very same people praying for my demise. I was under the assumption that the big homies had my best interest at heart, that they wanted me to be safe and to prosper. I could not have been more wrong about ANYTHING! The older cats in my neighborhood were out for self. As young drug dealers, my friends and I were nothing more than pawns being manipulated and moved into positions that benefitted others more than ourselves. We did not really mind getting the crumbs off their table, because the crumbs kept us satisfied at the time.

As a drug dealer, you will receive advice from dealers who have been at it much longer than you. They will share tricks of the trade and deliver these bits of information as though they are priceless gems, which explains why in street terminology wise advice is called a gem. These older hustlers share their experiences with you in hopes of impressing you because their self-esteem is based solely on how others view them, hence the flashy material possessions.

What drug dealers fail to realize is that the older dealers envy the younger ones because the younger ones do things differently. The older the dealer, the more cautious he is. While the younger dealers move boldly and with much less fear, utilizing the "greater risk-greater reward" approach. Older, more reserved hustlers are envious because they themselves lack the courage necessary to take big chances and put everything on the line time and time again. Older hustlers tend to operate in their personal comfort zone, rarely stepping outside of routines where they feel somewhat safe and secure. They would like to be more carefree, but they can't because they've been conditioned to move with caution. So when they see younger dealers moving recklessly and receiving larger pieces of the proverbial pie, the older dealers become jealous because they don't have the heart to go that far out on a limb.

Once the younger dealers make a bad move, the older ones actually applaud their downfall, whether openly or in secret behind closed doors. They never wanted to see the young dealers come up, because it would mean that they themselves got passed up and it would be a major blow to their already fragile egos. It can best be described as the "Crabs-in-a-bucket" effect. You can put multiple crabs in the same bucket and never have to worry about a single one of them getting out because as soon as one makes it near the top, one of the others will immediately pull it back down into the bucket. Poverty breeds crab-like individuals!

So drug dealers in general are selfish, egotistical, and envious of one another. Older dealers have it more than younger ones. This translates into fake praise when things appear to be going well for others, and false sympathy when things take a turn for the worst. In other words, they really hate to see anyone excel, but love to see them fail, because they feel as if nobody deserves success selling drugs if they don't have it first, and if they don't have more of it than everybody else.

Nobody told me any of this, so I grew up respecting men who had nothing but ill-will and larceny in their hearts when it came to me. No matter how much money I made for them, they never wanted to see me rise above them financially or otherwise. They basically wanted me to idolize them and look up to them for the things they had accomplished in the past, forgetting that tomorrow is always a new day full of new opportunities, even in the streets. Still, I understand where the envy comes from because I often felt it when I saw young hustlers enter the joint and live good off of the money that they had stacked up while selling drugs. It's as though each successive generation of drug dealers makes more money than the generation that preceded them. My generation is no exception, nor is the generation that came up under mine.

Chapter 8: "There's A Possibility You'll End Up A Murder Victim Or A Murderer!

Nobody bothered to tell me that my decision to sell drugs would mean that I had also signed up for the possibility of extreme violence. I still vividly recall when I started carrying a gun regularly. I had began to make a little more money than I was accustomed to making and a few thirsty eyes were watching me from a distance. I needed them to know that if they came for me, they had better be prepared to go all out, because I was not about to lay down without a fight.

As a drug dealer, there will be times when you have to let it be known that you are not an easy target. As you make more money and the wolves get wind of it, you may feel the need to protect yourself by carrying a gun. The problem with that is that when you have a gun in your possession, you conduct yourself very differently from when you do not have one on you. With a gun tucked in your waist, you may not be as quick to avoid conflict. Without it, you probably consider peaceful solutions.

By carrying a gun, you run the risk of using it. That means that a simple argument that could have been avoided can just as easily turn into a murder scene. As a drug dealer, you didn't sign up for unnecessary drama, beef, or war, yet you understand that it comes with the territory some time. When you're in the streets hustling, you run the risk of encountering and/or perpetuating some form of violence from time to time.

When you're getting enough money to attract the attention of vicious robbers, you may find yourself looking down the barrel of a gun that's being held by someone who has no conscience. This can be an extremely frightening feeling because nobody wants to give up their life over drugs or drug money, not for real. Yet the decision to sell drugs opens up the door for these types of situations to arise, ad in the blink of an eye the trigger can be squeezed and your life can come to a sudden end. That is a harsh reality!

On the other hand, by carrying a gun, you may find yourself aiming it at someone who has either wronged you, threatened you, or merely angered you. In a split second you can apply pressure to the trigger and quickly send a bullet through that person's head or heart, causing death immediately. And just that quickly you have become a bonafied murderer, despite the fact that you only started selling drugs because of your fascination with the fast money and other nonviolent things that accompanied drug dealing. Yet and still, a decision that took less than 10 seconds to make has suddenly changed your life forever and placed you beyond the empathy of normal people. You are now looked at with fear and contempt, as you should be. You see, sometimes you are on the right side of the gun, but it only takes one single time to end up on the wrong side of it and then the party is over.

Nobody told me any of this, so I developed a lack of respect for human life and forgot that no man has the right to decide whether another man lives or dies. Just because I am capable of ending a life, that does not mean I actually should go through with it when the circumstances contain that option. I did not comprehend this until it was too late and now I find myself trying to make amends while knowing deep in my heart that nothing I ever do can make up for the damage that I've done. That's a bitter pill to swallow because not a day goes by when I do not wonder if all of the pain I encounter is the direct result of my decision to cause pain to others by taking a man's life. I have never truly been able to come to terms with what I did, regardless of the circumstances that led up to it. When everything is said and done, my decision to sell drugs set the stage for me to become a convicted murder and to sacrifice my entire youth to the penal system. So yes, I fully know what it is like to sign up for one thing and inadvertently become something else along the way, because I experienced it firsthand and I am still dealing with the consequences!

Chapter 9: "Drugs Sell Themselves, So Everyone Is Disposable!"

Nobody bothered to tell me that my decision to sell drugs would eventually prove that I did not really matter in the grand scheme of things when it came to drug trafficking. I always felt like the streets needed me, the hood needed me, and the game needed me. Then I went to prison and realized just how little I was needed. The streets continued to function without me, the hood continued to survive without me, and the game continued to exist without me. In my absence, everything was business as usual.

As a drug dealer, you can pump up a block, lock up a strip, ad even flood an entire neighborhood. But the moment you disappear for whatever reason, it quickly becomes business as usual. There's always someone waiting in the wings to replace you and to do what you were doing, often better than you were doing it. You may think that you did something unique and unforgettable, but I assure you that is not the case. There is nothing new under the sun, so whatever you did had already been done before in some way, shape, fashion, or form, and it will eventually be done again.

Drug trafficking evolves and adapts to changing times. The participants may change, the process may change, but the act itself remains the same. As long as there is a way for people to get high, someone will find a way to profit from selling it, and someone will find a way to escape reality by purchasing it. Sellers and buyers are not going anywhere because poverty gives birth to, and fuels, addiction.

The thing about crack is that it doesn't take much to sell it. All you have to do is decide what you want for it, let it be known, and wait for the addict to accept or reject your terms. If they accept the terms, you have a completed drug transaction. If they reject the terms, you have to negotiate new terms or simply agree to part ways. That does not require much at all besides a little bit of your time and a small amount of patience.

So why is it that so many young dealers believe that the streets will suffer if they are removed from them, whether it be through incarceration or death? The answer is simple: They are delusional! If they were to look at the situation realistically, they would see that they are as disposable as the containers that they hold their drugs in. If they get arrested today, their most loyal customers will have a replacement dealer before the sun comes up tomorrow. There is no such thing as an irreplaceable drug dealer, never has been and never will be.

Nobody told me any of this, so I went through my teen years under the impression that I was needed in the streets. Once I got removed from those very same streets and saw how quickly my presence was forgotten, I understood just how insignificant my contributions were. In fact, my contributions had such a negative impact on my community that my removal was actually a good thing. Although others quickly stepped up to fill the void that I left, that void was small and easily filled. It does not require much to be an instrument of destruction in the hood, any fool could do it. Just look at me if you have any doubts!

Chapter 10: "The Dope Game Is Not A Game At All, It's A Trap!"

Nobody bothered to tell me that my decision to sell drugs would expose the fact that I was *playing* in the midst of some extremely serious shit. Since I was so young when I started selling drugs, I often found myself in grown man situations even though I was really just a child. I was not physically, mentally, emotionally, or spiritually equipped to handle those situations but I somehow managed to fake my way through most of them. And when I could not fake, I simply stood tall, as best I could and let the chips fall where they may.

When you become a drug dealer, you become a part of what is often referred to as the "Dope Game." What's ironic is the fact that it is not a game at all, because when you really think about it, nobody comes out a winner. Games have winners and losers, but everyone who gets into the dope game loses something, whether it be their life, their freedom, or just their innocence. So how is it a game?

What I have discovered is that the dope game is not a game, it is a trap. Perhaps that's why selling drugs has come to be known as "Trapping", drug spots are referred to as "Trap Houses", rap music that promotes drug dealing is called "Trap Rap", and drug dealers are labeled "Trappers." It seems like such an appropriate alternative since drug dealing is actually nothing more than a trap anyway.

Just think of an old school mouse trap, the one made of wood and the metal spring contraption that snaps around to break the mouse's neck when he starts nibbling on the cheese. The dope game reminds me of that because it lures mice in with the promise of cheese, only to set them up for the kill once they take the bait. So many young people in this day and age lack the courage to exercise discipline and stay away from destructive activities like drug dealing. These young people are more like frightened little mice than confident men, so they go after the cheese that has been strategically placed on the trap. The entire contraption is designed to end the mouse's life in one way or another. Once the weight of the trap bears down on his neck, he either dies instantly or he dies slowly. Either way, he dies!

Nobody told me any of this, so I ended up going after the cheese because at the time I was more mouse than man. I took pride in being a player in the dope game, never recognizing the fact that I had already lost before I even got started. Although the trap snapped down on my neck with enough force to end my life, I was fortunate and blessed to stay alive long enough to escape the trap and begin the healing process!

Conclusion

It is now my hope that what I have shared in these few pages can be used to help young people avoid some of the pitfalls that I fell into and that many of my peers fell victim to. There is no foolproof solution to the problems that they face as the next generation, but we have to each do what we can to provide them with various tools to ensure their survival. This is part of my effort and I pray that after reading it you will be encouraged and motivated to share some of this information with a young person who needs to hear it.

May God Bless You and Keep You!

Conclusion